TRAVELLING
WILD
TPB09-5

JOURNEY ALONG THE RIVER NILE

Sonya Newland

WAYLAND
www.waylandbooks.co.uk

First published in Great Britain in 2016
by Wayland

Copyright © Wayland, 2016

All rights reserved.
ISBN: 978 0 7502 9861 2
10 9 8 7 6 5 4 3 2 1

Wayland
An imprint of
Hachette Children's Group
Part of Hodder & Stoughton
Carmelite House
50 Victoria Embankment
London EC4Y 0DZ

An Hachette UK Company
www.hachette.co.uk

www.hachettechildrens.co.uk

A catalogue for this title is available from
the British Library

Printed and bound in Malaysia

 Produced for Wayland by
White-Thomson Publishing Ltd
www.wtpub.co.uk

Author: Sonya Newland
Designer: Rocket Design (East Anglia) Ltd
Picture researcher: Izzi Howell
Map: Stefan Chabluk
Wayland editor: Elizabeth Brent

Picture credits:

P5 Blaz Kure/Shutterstock; P6 Pecold/
Shutterstock; P7T Lingbeek/iStock; P7B
Ivan Vdovin/Alamy; P8 Greenshoots
Communications/Alamy; P9T Oleg
Znamenskiy/Shutterstock; P9B Albie
Venter/Shutterstock; P10 Naypong/
Shutterstock; P11T EcoPrint/Shutterstock;
P11M Julian W/Shutterstock; P11B Ryan
M. Bolton/Shutterstock; P12 BrettCharlton/
iStock; P13T Steve White-Thomson/White-
Thomson Publishing; P13B George Steinmetz/
Corbis; P14 ITAR-TASS Photo Agency/Alamy;
P15T Les Gibbon/Alamy; P15B Blickwinkel/
Alamy; P16 John Warburton-Lee Photography/
Alamy; P17T Michael Freeman/Corbis;
P17B Nonlani/Shutterstock; P18 Alexander
Kuguchin/Shutterstock; P19T Martchan/
Shutterstock; P19B BrianWancho/Shutterstock;
P20T MarcPo/iStock; P20B Werner Otto/
Alamy; P21 WitR/Shutterstock; P22T
Anton_Ivanov/Shutterstock; P22B Waupee/
iStock; P23 Lloyd Cluff/Corbis; P24 antpkr/
Shutterstock; P25T Lisa S./Shutterstock; P25B
R.M. Nunes/Shutterstock; P26 mikdam/iStock;
P27T sculpies/Shutterstock; P27B NASA/
Corbis; P28 Riaan van den Berg/Shutterstock;
P29T RiumaLab /Shutterstock; P29B Anton_
Ivanov/Shutterstock.

CONTENTS

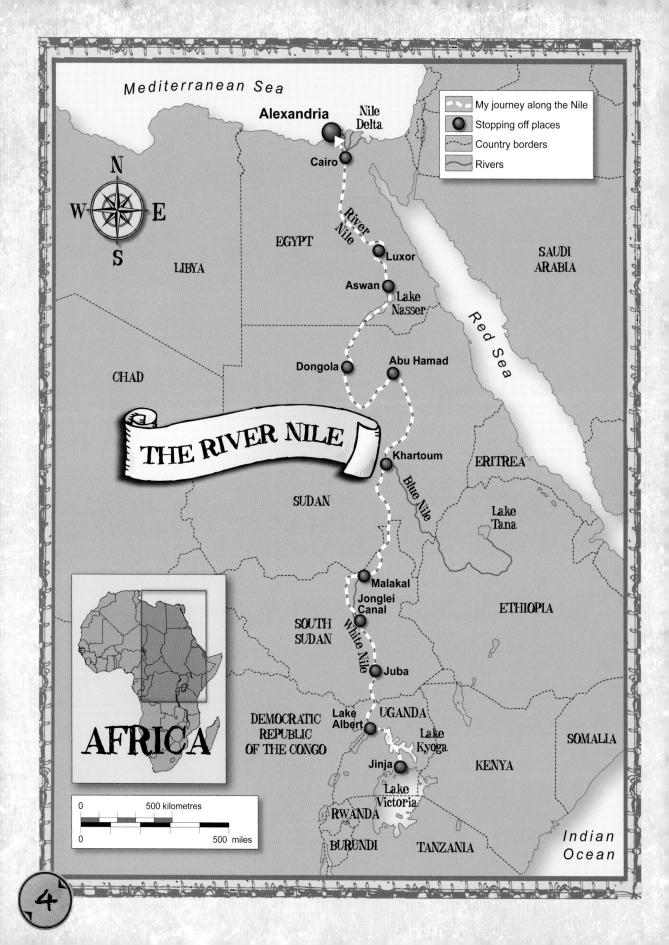

THE RIVER NILE

Preparing for the trip

It feels like I've been waiting forever, but at last the day is here! I'm finally setting off on my amazing journey up the River Nile (see map opposite). I'll be sailing in a traditional boat called a felucca, making camp at night on the banks of the river. There'll be some challenges along the way, including crocodiles, blood–sucking mosquitoes and who knows what else, but I'm really excited. It's going to be an awesome experience!

~~The longest river~~

The mighty Nile is the longest river in the world, stretching 6,650 km. The main parts of the Nile run though the countries of Uganda, South Sudan, Ethiopia, Sudan and Egypt, but smaller waterways feed into the river from other countries, too. Most rivers flow southwards, but the Nile flows northwards. It has several sources — the one furthest south is in Burundi. It eventually flows out into the Mediterranean Sea, north of the Egyptian capital, Cairo.

Climate

The Nile cuts its course through the deserts of north–eastern Africa, so I've planned my journey to avoid the blistering heat of summer. Throughout June and July, temperatures here soar to 40 °C and above, so I've chosen the cooler months of January through to March for my trip. With an average temperature of around 26 °C, it will still be warm and sunny — and even in winter I probably won't get caught in a downpour in this desert environment!

Equipment

I've decided to bring along the following:

- waterproof clothing
- insect repellent
- life jacket
- sunglasses
- water bottle
- rubber shoes
- map and compass
- binoculars
- hand fan
- sun cream
- sun hat
- matches
- hunting knife

SOURCES OF THE NILE

8 January
Jinja, Lake Victoria

This morning I flew into Kampala in Uganda to begin my great Nile journey. From the airport I headed straight out to the town of Jinja, which lies on the north shore of Lake Victoria, about 80 km east of the capital. I'm sitting here now on a jetty, watching the sun set over this vast expanse of water, wondering what adventures lie in store for me.

Lake Victoria

Lake Victoria is the largest lake in Africa. It covers an area of nearly 70,000 square km and straddles three countries: Kenya, Tanzania and Uganda. I chose the shoreside town of Jinja as my starting point because it lies close to the source of the White Nile, which I'll be following northwards. Many rivers and streams flow into Lake Victoria, including the Kagera River — another of the Nile's sources.

Be smart, survive!

Whenever you're travelling in a hot country, it's important to be aware of the dangers of the sun and the heat. Carry a water bottle with you at all times and drink from it frequently to stop yourself getting dehydrated and falling ill with heatstroke. Cover yourself in sun cream, wear a hat and stay out of the sun in the middle of the day.

The White Nile

There are different parts to the River Nile. The White Nile is the longest section, and its main source is at Lake Victoria. This shallow, wide part of the river flows for about 2,000 km. Many swamps lie on either side of the White Nile, where papyrus reeds grow.

The Blue Nile

The second main tributary of the river is the Blue Nile. The source of the Blue Nile is Lake Tana in Ethiopia. From there it winds westwards and then north—west to Khartoum in Sudan, where it meets the White Nile. The Blue Nile is so—called because of all the silt in the water, which turns it a very dark colour.

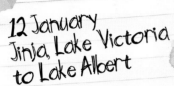

12 January
Jinja, Lake Victoria
to Lake Albert

I've been on the water for a few days and I'm getting used to it at last! It's not the most comfortable way to travel, but the scenery has been spectacular. This first part of my journey has taken me from Lake Victoria, through Lake Kyoga and onto Lake Albert. These three large bodies of water are all part of the group of lakes that lie in the region of the Upper Nile.

Ugandan children bring cattle to drink from the waters of Lake Albert.

Lakes of the southern Nile

The Great Lakes is the name given to the system of inland seas that stretches across six countries, from the Great Rift Valley in Kenya in the east to the Democratic Republic of Congo in the west. There are actually 15 lakes across this region, but only eight of them are classed as 'great', based on their size. These include Lake Victoria and Lake Albert in Uganda.

Lake Kyoga

At 130 km in length and less than 4 m deep in most places, Lake Kyoga isn't one of the official Great Lakes. However, the Nile flows through it on its way from Lake Victoria to Lake Albert, making it part of this complicated system of waterways. Kyoga is an important ecosystem, home to plants such as water lilies and papyrus, nearly 50 species of fish and reptiles such as crocodiles.

Murchison Falls

I decided to take time on dry land to explore Uganda's largest conservation area – Murchison Falls National Park, near Lake Albert. The Nile flows in a series of rapids through the park, before becoming the Murchison Falls and plummeting into the valley below. There's an amazing variety of wildlife here, including elephants and buffalo, as well as many beautiful birds.

Hippo attack!

With their sharp teeth and their ability to run surprisingly fast, hippos are among the most dangerous animals you'll encounter along the Nile. They will usually only attack a human if they feel threatened, so don't approach them on land and try not to run into one in your boat. If a hippo charges at you – run! It will probably give up the chase before it can catch you, but to be sure, weave between trees or rocks. This will make it harder for the hippo to corner you.

GET OUT ALIVE!!

RIVER REPTILES

18 January
Lake Albert to Juba, South Sudan

One thing I've learnt over the past few days is that the Nile can be a dangerous place! As I sailed across the border from Uganda towards Juba, the capital of South Sudan, I saw several crocodiles gliding through the water towards my boat. I was glad to be safely on deck, but as one of these fearsome-looking creatures snapped its deadly jaws at me, it still felt a bit too close for comfort!

River crocodiles

Nile crocodiles are the largest crocodiles in Africa, growing up to 6 m long and weighing as much as 680 kg. These crocs mainly eat fish, but they will also attack and kill animals that come to the river to drink at the water's edge. Nile crocodiles have been known to attack humans, too. Some experts think that around 200 people a year are killed by Nile crocodiles.

Nile monitors

Crocodiles aren't the only reptiles that live in and around the Nile. Venturing ashore one evening, I saw a giant lizard called a Nile monitor. These creatures can grow up to 2 m long, and they certainly look scary. However, they won't attack humans. Nile monitors prefer to feed on crocodile eggs.

Be smart, survive!

There are around ten species of venomous snake found in the regions along the Nile, including cobras and adders. Before I set off on my journey, I found out which snakes could prove deadly and which ones were harmless. It's always a good idea to look up the creatures you might come across on your travels so you can stay away from any that could be dangerous!

Turtles

African softshell turtles are some of the strangest-looking creatures to live in the waters of the Nile. Instead of the hard, bony scales that most turtles have, softshells have a flat, skin-like shell. They also have longer snouts than other turtles, which they use as a kind of snorkel to breathe while lying in the mud or shallow water at the river's edge.

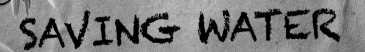

SAVING WATER

23 January
Juba to the Jonglei Canal

As I continue my journey northwards, I start to notice many people along the riverbanks, using the water for washing their clothes (and themselves!) and carrying it away for drinking and cooking. The river is clearly an important part of their lives, but I can see that pollution and other environmental issues are a big problem.

Industry and agriculture

Both industry and agriculture have contributed to polluting the Nile. Chemicals used in farming, such as pesticides, and even natural materials such as salts and nutrients, all damage the river environment. There are also many factories along the river, and polluted waste water from these is disposed of in the Nile.

Water pollution

The effect of water pollution is widespread. Local people use water from the Nile, but the chemicals and waste in it make it unpleasant and even dangerous to drink. Pollution is also harming the fish and other creatures that live in and around the Nile, which in turn affects the fishermen who depend on the river for their livelihood.

Be smart, survive!

Never drink water straight from the river - it is filled with pollutants. You can buy portable water filters or chemical tablets that will purify water when you're travelling wild. Alternatively, boiling the water will get rid of many impurities and make the water safer to drink. It's always wise to take a good supply of bottled water with you.

The drop in numbers of fish in the Nile is making it harder for fishermen to earn a living.

The Jonglei Canal

The land the Nile flows through is desert, with hardly any rainfall. Conserving water and finding ways to get it to people who live further away from the river is important. The Jonglei Canal was intended to carry Nile water to wider parts of Egypt and Sudan. Unfortunately, the project was stopped before the canal was completed.

NILE FISH

30 January
Jonglei Canal to Malakal

I've spent the past few days sailing leisurely towards the city of Malakal in South Sudan, where the Nile meets the Sobat River. Up to now I've lived off supplies bought along the way, but today I decided to try out my survival skills and see if I could catch a fish for my dinner. It took a lot of patience, but I've just finished a delicious meal of Nile perch that I caught myself!

Nile perch

The famous Nile perch is one of the largest freshwater fish in the world. Some can grow to 2 m long and weigh up to 200 kg! It feeds on other fish, insects and molluscs. But the Nile perch is itself an important food in this part of Africa and you'll find it on the menu of all local restaurants. There are still plenty of perch in the Nile, but fishermen worry about the numbers declining, as this could badly affect the local economy.

Other fish

There are more than 100 species of fish in the Nile and its lakes.

• The giant tigerfish is known as the 'piranha of Africa'. It has strong jaws and extremely sharp teeth. It preys on most other species of fish — there are even reports of giant tigerfish attacking people!

• Lungfish, such as the marbled lungfish, can grow up to 2 m long. They are unique in the fish world because they have lungs, which allow them to breathe in water that does not have much oxygen in it, such as swamps and floodplains.

• There are several catfish species in the Nile. The Nile catfish is sometimes known as the 'upside down' catfish because it swims on its back! Catfish will eat almost anything — including rubbish that finds its way into the river.

Be smart, survive!

You can make a simple fishing rod using a stick and a piece of long grass or a reed as the fishing line. Tie two or more reeds together if you need to. You can carve a hook from a twig or use a piece of wire if you have some. Tie the reeds to the stick, then attach a small pebble close to the bottom of the line as a weight. Attach the hook to the bottom, bait it and cast your line into the river!

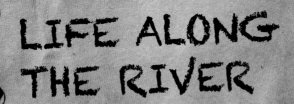

LIFE ALONG
THE RIVER

9 February
Malakal to Khartoum, Sudan

The journey from Malakal to Khartoum was the longest stretch of the river I've travelled in one go and I'm happy to be spending a few days on land again. Khartoum is one of the largest cities along the Nile, so I'd expected it to be busy – there's so much going on here! I've had a brilliant day exploring the markets and museums, listening to the melodic calls to prayer from the minarets.

People of the Nile

Just as in ancient times, the main population centres in eastern Africa are located in the Nile Valley, on the banks of the river. Settlements grew up here because the river provided a vital source of water, land for farming, food and a means of getting from one place to another. The Nile runs through several different countries, so the people who live along its banks have many different customs and traditions according to the history of their own nation. However, the river is a source of life for all of them.

Khartoum

The sprawling capital of Sudan is located at the point where the Blue Nile and the White Nile meet. From here, they combine to form one river and journey northwards to the Mediterranean Sea. About five million people live in this busy city. High—rise office buildings sit alongside traditional mosques, and businessmen and women in suits walk to work through historic souks.

Religion

As in most African countries, Sudan's population is mostly Muslim. There are also small numbers of Christians and people who follow traditional African beliefs. There are many beautiful mosques in towns and cities across the region. A lot of them have minarets, or tall towers, nearby. From these towers, a man called a muezzin cries out to let Muslims know it is time to pray. He does this five times a day — at dawn, midday, mid—afternoon, sunset and nightfall. The muezzin then leads the people in prayer.

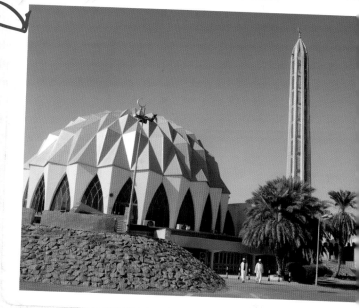

DESERT LANDSCAPE

16 February
Khartoum to Abu Hamad

I've stopped at the town of Abu Hamad to calm my nerves! I'd grown used to the gentle waters of the Nile, so it was a complete surprise to suddenly find myself trying to keep the boat steady through a series of fast-flowing rapids. I later discovered that these are called cataracts – and I'm going to have to find my way through more of them before my journey's end!

Nile cataracts

The cataracts are a series of white-water rapids along the part of the Nile between Khartoum and Aswan, in Egypt. Here the water is shallow, with boulders and rocks sticking out of the surface. This makes the river treacherous to navigate. There are six cataracts in all and some of them are only passable by boat during the flood season, when the Nile waters are at their highest.

The Great Bend

For most of its course, the Nile flows northwards. At Abu Hamad, however, it changes direction and flows south-west, away from the sea. It runs for more than 300 km before heading north again, creating a great s-shaped bend in the river. This change of direction is caused by tectonic plates – vast pieces of the earth's crust. These move very slowly, grinding past each other, changing some of our planet's surface features.

The Nubian Desert

The Great Bend of the Nile takes a winding course through the Nubian Desert. The landscape here is rocky rather than sandy, and is cut through with dry riverbeds known as wadis. These fill with water during occasional sudden downpours, but they dry up before the water ever reaches the Nile.

Keeping away mosquitoes

GET OUT ALIVE!!

Insects thrive on and around rivers such as the Nile. Most are just annoying but some, such as mosquitoes, can spread diseases. To avoid being bitten, always wear insect repellent. Protect yourself by covering your arms and legs so your skin isn't exposed. Insects like evenings, so if you're sitting outside at nightfall, light a camp fire and the smoke will keep them at a distance. Taking malaria tablets can stop you getting ill if you are bitten.

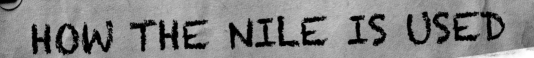

21 February
Abu Hamad to
Dongola, Sudan

I spent an amazing day today at Dongola, one of the main sites of the Nubian people. All around this region are archaeological remains of the ancient Nubian civilisation, especially at Old Dongola, about 80 km from the city. Watching all the comings and goings on the Nile got me thinking about the many ways in which people use this mighty waterway.

Commercial waterway

The Nile is a major transportation route in this part of Africa. The people here travel from place to place by boat, especially during the flood season when many roads are impassable. Several canals have been built along the route of the Nile, too. These are an important means of transporting goods to centres further away from the river.

Fishing

Catching and selling fish is a major industry in the Nile Valley. Many fishermen have homes along the banks of the river, but some live on their boats on the river itself. There are strict rules about the type and numbers of fish that can be caught in the Nile. Police patrol parts of the river to make sure the fishermen aren't breaking these rules.

Be smart, survive!

The ancient Egyptians used spears or nets to catch fish. You can weave a net from willow branches or long reeds if you can find them, then have two people stand in the river holding each end of the net so that the main part of it is under the water. To make your own spear, find a medium-length – but strong – branch and bind your hunting knife to the end of it. Stand very still and quietly in shallow water until you see a fish, then spear it quickly. You'll need good reflexes!

Tourism

The tourist trade is extremely important to the economy of East Africa. In the Nile Valley, more than 80 per cent of people who have jobs work in the tourist industry. They cater to the thousands of visitors who flock to Egypt every year to see the ancient temples and pyramids. Nile cruises are also a popular tourist attraction, taking sightseers on trips to major historical sites, sometimes on traditional boats called feluccas, like mine.

THE RIVER IN FLOOD

2 March
Dongola to Aswan

I had to survive several more cataracts before I finally reached the great blue expanse of Lake Nasser, in southern Egypt. At more than 5,000 square km, Nasser is the second-largest artificial lake in the world – and it's quite a sight to see! The lake was formed when the Aswan High Dam was built in the middle of the twentieth century. Today it is a popular spot for perch-fishing, so I spent an enjoyable afternoon with my fishing line again!

Be smart, survive!

Even in the desert it can get cold at night, so when I'm camping on shore I build a fire in the evening. This not only keeps me warm, but also keeps away insects and other animals that might get too close! I gather dry sticks and pile them into a pyramid shape, and I collect dry grass and reeds to put in the middle to help the fire light. I brought matches with me to make it easy to start the fire.

Nile floods

In the past, every year between June and September, rain and melting snow from the mountains in Ethiopia sent a rush of water down the Nile. This made the river overflow and flood the surrounding area, depositing a rich silt all along its banks. The silt made the soil ideal for growing crops and allowed the great civilisation of the ancient Egyptians to flourish. They called the river 'Ar' ('black') because of this silt. However, the Nile floods were not always good news. In years when the floods were very high, crops could be washed away. In years with low floods, crops could fail through drought.

The Aswan Dam

The 111 m-high Aswan High Dam was built in 1970 to control the flooding of the Nile. Thousands of people lived along this stretch of the Nile and they had to move to make way for the dam and the lake it made. This was difficult for many of them, whose families had settled there for generations. There was also great concern that the building of the dam and the lake would damage the ancient temples of Abu Simbel. In the end, these magnificent buildings were carefully removed and rebuilt further away.

23

AN ANCIENT CIVILISATION

6 March
Aswan to Luxor

Along the banks of the river between Aswan and Luxor are some of the most impressive ruins of the ancient Egyptian civilisation. I've wandered amongst enormous temples and imposing statues, huge carved obelisks and pillars that seem to support the sky itself. Along the way, I've learnt more about the people who made their homes on the banks of the Nile thousands of years ago.

The ancient Egyptians

The civilisation of ancient Egypt was only able to grow and become great because of the River Nile. The first settlers here farmed the land, growing important crops such as wheat for food, flax for clothing and papyrus reeds to make a type of paper. The ancient Egyptians based their calendar around the seasons of the Nile: Akhet (the flood season), Peret (the growing season) and Shemu (the harvest).

The tissue in the stems of the papyrus plant can be dried to create a material for writing on.

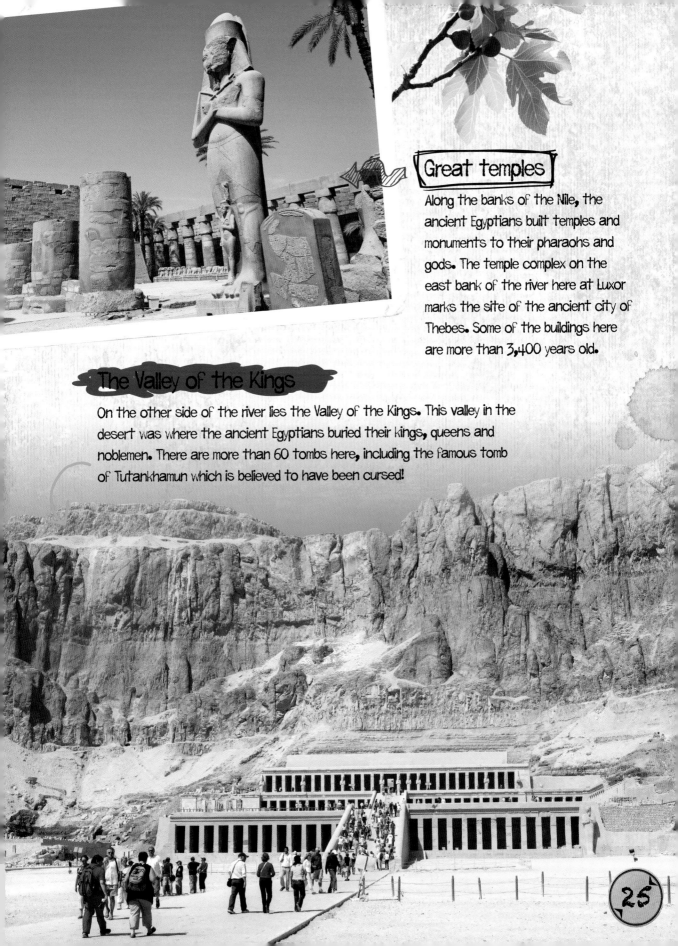

Great temples

Along the banks of the Nile, the ancient Egyptians built temples and monuments to their pharaohs and gods. The temple complex on the east bank of the river here at Luxor marks the site of the ancient city of Thebes. Some of the buildings here are more than 3,400 years old.

The Valley of the Kings

On the other side of the river lies the Valley of the Kings. This valley in the desert was where the ancient Egyptians buried their kings, queens and noblemen. There are more than 60 tombs here, including the famous tomb of Tutankhamun which is believed to have been cursed!

THE NILE DELTA

16 March
Luxor to Cairo

I'm nearly at the end of my Nile adventure, but before I head off, I decided to spend a few days in Cairo – a hub of Egyptian culture and tourism. I love the buzz of the city, but I also couldn't miss the chance to travel into the desert to see the awe-inspiring pyramids at Giza, before setting sail once more into the Nile Delta and towards my final destination.

Cairo

The city that grew to become the capital of Egypt was established more than 1,000 years ago. Since then it has become the heart of the country's cultural and religious life. It can seem too busy and crowded in Cairo sometimes, particularly as there are thousands of tourists in the main streets and marketplaces. But a wander through some of the back streets will give you a glimpse of how people really live in one of Africa's greatest cities.

The pyramids

In the desert not far from Cairo stand the most famous monuments from the ancient world – the pyramids at Giza. Of the three pyramids, the Great Pyramid is the largest and the oldest. This tomb for the pharaoh Khufu dates from around 2560 BCE and took around 20 years to build. Nearby stands the mysterious statue known as The Sphinx, with a lion's body and a pharaoh's head.

Creepy-crawlies

While I was spending a couple of days camping near the pyramids, my guide gave me a good tip for avoiding being bitten or stung by scorpions and other creepy-crawlies that live in the desert. Always shake out your sleeping bag before you climb into it at night to make sure nothing has crawled inside. And check your clothes and boots carefully before you put them on in the morning. A nip from some desert insects can be extremely painful – even deadly!

The Nile Delta

The Nile Delta is the huge area where the Nile fans out and flows into the Mediterranean Sea. It covers about 20,000 square km and stretches along 240 km of the Mediterranean coastline. The river splits into two branches here – the Rosetta and the Damietta. The soil in the delta is ideal for growing crops, so people have lived and farmed this area for thousands of years. Today, around half of Egypt's total population – 40 million people – live in the Nile Delta.

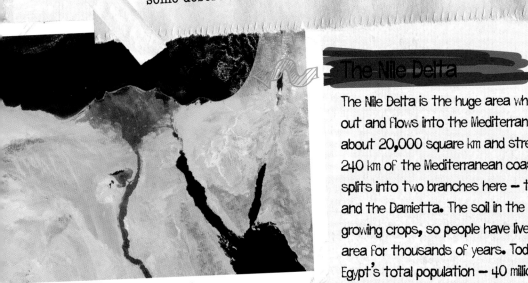

This satellite image shows how the Nile spreads in the delta region as it approaches the Meditteranean Sea.

JOURNEY'S END

20 March
Cairo to Alexandria

Well, here I am in the ancient city of Alexandria. I can't believe my journey has ended! I've had a fascinating final few days though, travelling through the Rosetta branch of the Nile Delta, where I had a chance to do some bird-watching. Before I catch my flight home, I'm also going to take a last look at some of the amazing ancient ruins that Egypt has to offer.

Delta birds

Due to its warm temperatures, the Nile Delta is a wintering place for hundreds of thousands of birds during their annual migration. In some of the more marshy lakes in the delta region you can see terns, wigeons, herons and coots. You might also catch sight of an ibis — a water bird honoured by the ancient Egyptians.

Alexandria

In ancient times, the port city of Alexandria was a great centre of learning and culture for the Egyptians. It was home to the greatest library in the ancient world, where scrolls and books were kept for scholars to read. It is thought that the old library was destroyed in around 390 CE, but a modern library has now been built in Alexandria to keep its legacy alive.

Saving the Nile

My journey up the Nile has been an extraordinary adventure. I've discovered loads about this important river and the people who rely on it. It's obviously vital to protect its waters so that it can continue to bring life to the Nile Valley — and to more distant parts of the desert — just as it has done for thousands of years.

GLOSSARY

artificial Made by humans.

conservation Protecting or restoring parts of the natural world that are under threat.

dam A barrier that stops the flow of water to create a reservoir, or store, of water.

dehydrated When you don't have enough water in your body, which can make you ill.

drought A period of unexpectedly low rainfall, which causes severe water shortages.

economy The system of how money is made and used in a particular country or region.

ecosystem All the plants and animals in a particular area.

felucca A traditional Egyptian sailing boat.

flax A flowering plant that is used to make a fibre for clothes.

floodplain The flattish land on either side of a river, which often floods after heavy rain.

impassable Blocked so that nothing can get through.

jetty A small raised platform on legs that sticks into a body of water, which boats can be tied to.

livelihood The way that people earn enough money to live.

migration The seasonal movement of birds and other animals between colder and warmer parts of the world.

minarets Towers linked to mosques from which criers call Muslims to prayer five times each day.

mollusc A group of animals that do not have backbones, including snails, slugs and octopuses. Most molluscs live in water.

nutrient A nourishing substance.

obelisk A tall, four-sided stone pillar, often carved with writing.

papyrus A plant that grows in water and can be used to make a material for writing on.

pesticide A chemical sprayed on plants and crops to keep away insects and animals that might harm them.

pharaoh A king or queen in ancient Egypt.

pollution Chemicals or rubbish that have a negative effect on soil, air, water or other parts of the environment.

rapids Stretches of shallow, fast-flowing water where the surface is often broken by rocks and boulders.

reptile A cold-blooded animal that lays eggs.

silt Fine sand, clay or rock particles that are carried by running water.

souk An open-air market.

swamp An area of low-lying, wet ground.

tectonic plates Huge sections of the earth beneath its surface, which move very slowly.

treacherous Very dangerous.

tributary A river or stream that feeds into a larger river.

venomous Describes a creature such as a snake that can give you a poisonous bite or sting.

wadi A dried river or creek bed often found in deserts.

INDEX & FURTHER INFORMATION

Books

Journey Along a River: Nile by Paul Harrison (Wayland, 2013)
River Adventures: Nile by Paul Manning (Franklin Watts, 2014)
The Nile: River in the Sand (Rivers Around the World) by Molly Aloian
(Crabtree Publishing, 2010)

Websites

http://www.bbc.co.uk/history/ancient/egyptians/nile_01.shtml
http://www.historyforkids.net/river-nile.html
http://www.scienceforkidsclub.com/nile-river.html

OTHER TITLES IN THE TRAVELLING WILD SERIES

TREKKING THE SAHARA DESERT
9780750285841

JOURNEY ALONG THE RIVER NILE
9780750298612

CLIMBING THE HIMALAYAN MOUNTAINS
9780750298643

SAILING THE CARIBBEAN ISLANDS
9780750298650

JOURNEY ALONG THE AMAZON
9780750283052

TREKKING IN THE CONGO RAINFOREST
9780750283236

EXPEDITION TO THE ARCTIC
9780750283243

SAILING THE GREAT BARRIER REEF
9780750283250